Contents

Features 2

Unit 1: Dictionary Skills
Dictionary Entries Diagram 3
Learning About Dictionary Entries 4
Reviewing Proper Nouns 5
Reviewing Pronouns 6
Reviewing Verbs 7
Reviewing Adjectives 8
Reviewing Adverbs 9
Reviewing Contractions 10
Reviewing Prefixes and Root Words 11
Reviewing Suffixes and Root Words 12
Using a Pronunciation Guide 13
Words with Multiple Meanings 14
Using Guide Words and Entry Words 15
Using a Dictionary 16
Show What You Know 17

Unit 2: Resources
News Article 18
Brochure 22
Almanac 26
Advertisement 30
Web Site 34

Unit 3: Text Features
Title Page/Copyright Page 38
Table of Contents 41
Headings and Captions 44
Index 47

Unit 4: Visual Features
Chart 50
Map 54
Diagram 58

Answer Key 62

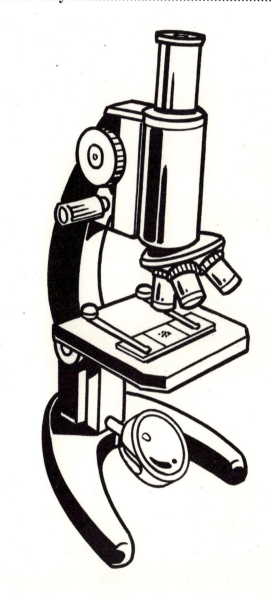

HMH Supplemental Publishers Inc. is not responsible for the content of any Web site listed in this book except its own. All material contained on these sites is the responsibility of the hosts and creators. The Web site addresses are current as of the date of publication.

Features

Using Information Resources is designed as a supplement to your curriculum. Throughout school and in life, students need to be able to look up information in various resources and use text and visual features to gain information. This product will introduce students to resources and features, and it will build their confidence in using resources independently.

Each lesson is set up in a similar way.

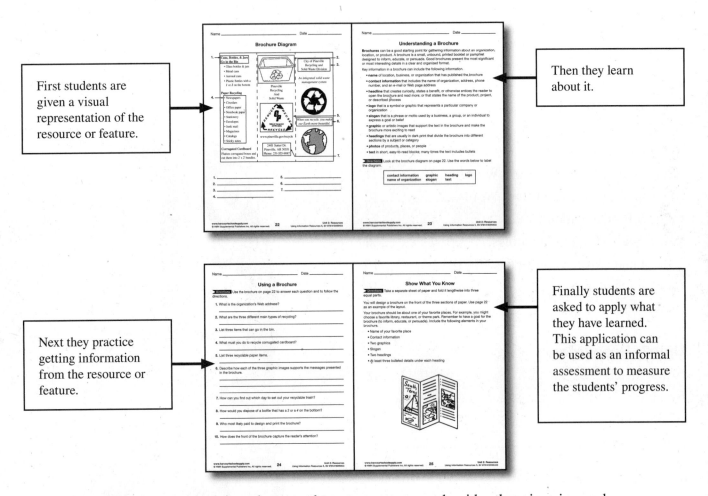

First students are given a visual representation of the resource or feature.

Then they learn about it.

Next they practice getting information from the resource or feature.

Finally students are asked to apply what they have learned. This application can be used as an informal assessment to measure the students' progress.

This step-by-step approach introduces students to resources and guides them in using each resource in a meaningful way so that they internalize how to use it and understand why it is helpful. The lessons in Unit 3 follow this same approach, but in a three-page format. The visual representation and information for learning are combined on one page.

Because a dictionary is so rich with information and so important to a student's learning, the unit on dictionaries is set like the other lessons in the product but includes additional practice. The unit begins with the visual representation and ends with application. The lessons in between provide specific practice with all of the skills needed to use a dictionary effectively.

We hope that students will have fun, be challenged, and enjoy using information resources to learn!

Dictionary Skills

Dictionary Entries Diagram

1. → **fogy   folly**

   fogy (fō′ gē) *n.* a person who is old-fashioned or highly conservative in ideas and actions.

   foi ble (foi′ bəl) *n.* 1. a small weakness; slight frailty in character. 2. the weakest part of a sword blade.

2. → **foil**[1] (foil) *v.* to keep from being successful. We tried to foil the burglar's plans. ← 3.

4. → **foil**[2] (foil) *n.* 1. a very thin sheet of metal. 2. a long, thin sword used for fencing. ← 5.

   fo li age (fō′ lē ij) *n.* leaves, as of a plant or tree.

   fo li ar (fō′ lē ər) *adj.* of or like a leaf or leaves.

6. → **fo li ate**[1] (fō′ lē āt) *v.* 1. to divide into thin layers. 2. to decorate with leaflike layers or ornamentation. 3. to number the leaves of a book.

   fo li ate[2] (fō′ lē āt) *adj.* 1. having or covered with leaves. 2. like a leaf or leaves.

   fo li ation (fō lē ā′ shən) *n.* 1. a growing of or developing into a leaf. 2. the state of being a leaf. 3. the way leaves are arranged inside a bud. 4. the process or beating metal into layers. 5. splitting into leaflike layers. 6. the process of backing glass to make a mirror. 7. the consecutive numbering of leaves. 8. a decoration with leaflike ornamentation.

7. → **fo lio** (fō′ lē ō) *n.* 1. a page or a ledger, or facing pages with the same number. 2. a set number of words considered as a unit of measuring the length of a legal or official document. 3. a large sheet of paper folded once, so that it forms two leaves, or four pages, of a book.

8. → **fo li ose** (fō′ lē ōs) *adj.* covered with leaves; leafy.

   fo lium (fō′ lē əm) *n.* 1. a thin layer of stratum, as in metamorphic rock. 2. the ← 9. looping, closed part of a curve extending from a node.

10. → **folk**[1] (fōk) *n.* people in general.

    folk[2] (fōk) *adj.* having to do with the common people.

    folky (fō′ kē) *adj.* of or having to do with folk music.

1. _____   6. _____
2. _____   7. _____
3. _____   8. _____
4. _____   9. _____
5. _____   10. _____

Learning About Dictionary Entries

A **dictionary** is a reference book that gives information about words. You can look at a dictionary to find out what a word means. You can also use a dictionary to check the spelling or pronunciation of a word or to figure out how to use the word in a sentence.

Each page of a dictionary has **guide words.** The guide words tell the first and last entry words that appear on a page. An **entry word** is a word that is defined. The dictionary entries diagram on page 3 has 17 entry words. Each entry word is in dark print. Each entry also shows how the word is broken into **syllables.** A syllable is a single unit of sound. In the word *operate,* the syllabication is op er ate. There are three syllables. The spaces show where each **syllable break** is.

Just after the entry word, the **part of speech** is given.
- An *n.* means the word is a noun.
- A *v.* means the word is a verb.
- An *adj.* means the word is an adjective.
- An *adv.* means the word is an adverb.
- A *prep.* means the word is a preposition.

Different words that are spelled the same way have tiny **raised numbers** at the end of the word. Here is an example.

- **alley**[1] (al′ē) *n.* a lane in a garden or park, bordered by trees or shrubs. She walked in the alley.
- **alley**[2] (al′ē) *n.* a fine marble used as the shooter in playing marbles. He used the alley to knock the last marble out of the ring.

The **pronunciation guide** helps the reader say the word. The pronunciation guide spells the word in a way that helps you sound it out. The spelling is in parentheses.

The **definition** tells what the word means. If there is more than one definition, they are numbered.

A **sample sentence** gives an example of how the entry word can be used. Each sample sentence is underlined in the diagram on page 3.

▶ **Directions** Look at the dictionary entries diagram on page 3. Use the words and definitions below to label the dictionary entries diagram.

definition	definition number
entry word (one syllable)	entry word (three syllables)
guide words	part of speech
pronunciation guide	raised number
sample sentence	syllable break

Name _____ Date _____

Reviewing Proper Nouns

A **noun** is a word that names a person, place, or thing.

There are two main types of nouns—**common nouns** and **proper nouns.** A common noun names any of a class of objects, such as girl, state, or author. A proper noun names a particular person, place, or thing. A proper noun, such as Abraham Lincoln, Tennessee, or Washington Monument, begins with a capital letter. The dictionary helps to determine whether nouns require capitalization or not.

▶ **Directions** Write a proper noun suggested by each common noun.

1. school _____
2. river _____
3. governor _____
4. singer _____
5. doctor _____
6. holiday _____
7. TV show _____
8. city _____
9. teacher _____
10. classmate _____
11. car _____
12. lake _____
13. country _____
14. street _____
15. monument _____
16. park _____
17. month _____
18. actor _____
19. girl _____
20. state _____

▶ **Directions** Write a common noun suggested by each proper noun.

21. Alaska _____
22. South America _____
23. Tuesday _____
24. Dr. Guerrero _____
25. Nile _____
26. Everest _____
27. *Harry Potter and the Sorcerer's Stone* _____
28. Mars _____
29. David _____
30. August _____

Name _____ Date _____

Reviewing Pronouns

A **pronoun** is a word that takes the place of one or more nouns.

Subject pronouns such as *I, we, you, he, she, it,* and *they* can be used as the subject of a sentence.

Nouns	**Subject Pronouns**
Marcy loves math.	*She* loves math.
Jon and Matt are funny.	*They* are funny.

▶ **Directions** Read each sentence. Write a subject pronoun that can take the place of the underlined word or words on each line.

1. Jenna, Mary, and I went to the store to buy more dog food. _____

2. Mike Ross is the new class president. _____

3. James left his lunch on the bus. _____

4. The book is called *Smart with Money*. _____

5. Where should Sue and Mark practice volleyball? _____

6. Is Samantha going to go to the movies? _____

7. The adult birds must make many trips each day to feed the babies. _____

The pronouns *me, you, him, her, it, us,* and *them* are **object pronouns**. Object pronouns come after verbs and words such as *to, for, in, at,* and *with*.

Nouns	**Object Pronouns**
Max said goodbye to *Linda*.	Max said goodbye to *her*.
The squirrel ate *the whole nut*.	The squirrel ate *it*.

▶ **Directions** Read each sentence. Write an object pronoun that can take the place of the underlined word or words.

8. Danny handed the popcorn to Emma. _____

9. Janet and James took turns playing with the puppy. _____

10. I will go to the counter to buy the hotdogs. _____

11. Ivanna helped John and Katie. _____

12. She said that she wanted to stay with Jack and me. _____

13. Jennifer told Roxanne about her plans. _____

14. Abbie gave Jonah and me her soccer ball. _____

Name _____ Date _____

Reviewing Verbs

An **action verb** is a word that shows action. An action verb tells what a person or thing does.

   Hogan *delivers* the newspaper on Mondays.
   Matilda *loves* cats.

Sometimes verbs have two parts, a **helping verb** followed by a **main verb**. Together, they are called a **verb phrase**. The helping verb does not show action.

   Mom *is going* to the store.
   Amelia *has eaten* most of her dinner.

Some other common helping verbs are *am, are, was, were, will, have,* and *had*.

A **linking verb** links the subject of a sentence with the word or words that describe the subject.

   Grandma *looked* happy to see us. (*happy* describes *Grandma*)
   Sam *is* still sleepy. (*sleepy* describes *Sam*)

Some other common linking verbs are *am, are, was, were, appear, will be, feel, smell, seem,* and *taste*.

▶ **Directions** Read each sentence and underline the **main verb**. Write *action* or *linking* on each line to tell what kind of verb it is.

1. You will be tired after the swim meet. _____
2. Sam guessed the ending of the book. _____
3. Marcia is sad that you won't be joining us. _____
4. James left his favorite book at school. _____
5. Monica and Jeff drove us to the football game. _____
6. The cookies tasted a little too salty. _____
7. Shanna feels bad that she hurt Matthew's feelings. _____
8. Jake will be mad when he hears about your plans. _____
9. The bouquet of flowers was very fragrant. _____
10. Scott sang songs to his brother, Stevie. _____
11. The restaurant smells like garlic. _____
12. Amy and her dad worked on the old bicycle. _____

Name _____   Date _____

Reviewing Adjectives

An **adjective** is a word that describes a noun or pronoun. An adjective can describe by comparing.

Most one-syllable adjectives usually use *er* or *est* to make comparisons. Use *est* to compare more than two persons or things.

   Miguel is *younger* than his brother.

Many adjectives of two or more syllables use *more* or *most* to make comparisons.

   Yesterday was the *most wonderful* day of Miguel's life.

▶ **Directions** Read each sentence. Write the correct form of the adjective in parentheses ( ) on the line.

1. Our trip to New Mexico was (wonderful) than I expected. _____
2. The mountains are the (beautiful) I have seen. _____
3. We saw Wheeler Peak, the (high) point in the state. _____
4. We visited a mine shaft that was (deep) than a mile. _____
5. Mining is one of the (big) industries in New Mexico. _____
6. Santa Fe, the state capital, is the (large) city in New Mexico. _____
7. It is also the (easy) city to reach by plane. _____
8. The (unusual) place we saw was Carlsbad Caverns. _____
9. We had never seen (strange) rocks than those. _____
10. To me, the (interesting) place of all was Santa Fe. _____
11. It is one of the (old) cities in North America. _____
12. Winters are (cold) there than in many northern cities. _____

▶ **Directions** On another sheet of paper, write ten adjectives that describe you. Then write five sentences that compare you to someone or something else.

Name _____ Date _____

Reviewing Adverbs

An **adverb** is a word that tells more about a verb.

Some adverbs tell *how quickly* an action takes place. Most of these end in *ly*.

   The train *slowly* pulled out of the station.

Some adverbs tell *when* an action takes place.

   The train left *yesterday*.

Some adverbs tell *where* an action takes place.

   We were *here* when it left.

| carefully | directly | everywhere | expertly | Finally | personally |
| professionally | Quickly | strangely | there | worriedly | |

▶ **Directions** Complete the sentences by adding words from the box that tell how, when, or where. The words in parentheses give a clue to the word to use.

1. I had looked _____ for my dog Tucker. (where)

2. I called to him _____. (how)

3. _____, Tucker came walking _____ toward me. (when, how)

4. I checked his leg _____ and saw that he was hurt. (how)

5. _____ we drove Tucker to the vet. (how)

6. We knew the vet _____. (how)

7. She was able to take Tucker _____ into the examining room. (how)

8. Tucker relaxed while he was _____. (where)

9. The vet handled my dog _____. (how)

10. She _____ cleaned and wrapped the wound. (how)

▶ **Directions** Choose a reading book from your desk or your school library. Find fifteen adverbs in the book and list them on another sheet of paper. If you are not sure if a word is an adverb, look in the dictionary.

Name _____ Date _____

Reviewing Contractions

A **contraction** is a shortened form of two words. An **apostrophe** takes the place of one or more letters. In the contraction *haven't*, the apostrophe takes the place of the letter *o*.

is not	isn't	they will	they'll
it is	it's	do not	don't
are not	aren't	does not	doesn't
was not	wasn't	did not	didn't
were not	weren't	could not	couldn't
has not	hasn't	should not	shouldn't
have not	haven't	would not	wouldn't
had not	hadn't	cannot	can't
he will	he'll		

▶ **Directions** Read each sentence. Look at the underlined words. Think of a contraction to use in place of the underlined words. Write the answer on the line.

1. Clint knows that <u>it is</u> important to eat a healthy diet. _____
2. <u>He will</u> try to eat more healthy foods. _____
3. Clint <u>is not</u> fond of vegetables. _____
4. Clint's body <u>cannot</u> grow stronger without these foods. _____

5. He <u>does not</u> have the energy he needs to play sports. _____
6. Clint <u>was not</u> always this fussy about what he ate. _____
7. His parents <u>are not</u> pleased with the change. _____
8. <u>They will</u> continue to offer Clint healthy foods in different ways. _____
9. His parents will make sure Clint <u>does not</u> eat junk foods. _____
10. Eventually, Clint <u>does not</u> eat junk foods; he craves healthy foods! _____

▶ **Directions** On another sheet of paper, write at least five sentences about something that you don't like to do. Use at least one contraction in each of your sentences. Circle the contractions that you use.

Reviewing Prefixes and Root Words

A **prefix** is added to the beginning of a word to change its meaning.

The nurse is available.   The doctor is *un*available.

The part of the word that a prefix is added to is called a **root word.**

*re*mark   *un*ruly

Prefix	Meaning	Example
dis	not	*dis*appear
im	not	*im*mature
in	not	*in*dependent
mis	incorrectly	*mis*name
bi	two	*bi*cycle
non	not	*non*sense
pre	before	*pre*test
re	again	*re*sent
re	back	*re*turn
un	not	*un*reliable
un	opposite of	*un*fold

▶ **Directions** Complete the chart by adding a prefix to the word. The new word should have the meaning listed in the second column. Use the list above to help you.

Prefix + Word	Meaning
1. _____view	view beforehand
2. _____fiction	not fiction
3. _____fund	to pay back
4. _____use	to use incorrectly
5. _____sure	not sure
6. _____satisfied	not satisfied

▶ **Directions** Read each sentence. Add the prefix to each word that makes the most sense. Use the list above to help you.

7. The Tyrannosaurus rex is a _____historic creature.

8. The sound of the hammer pounding was _____stop; I heard it all day.

9. If I don't understand what I have read, it helps me to _____read it.

Name _____ Date _____

Reviewing Suffixes and Root Words

A **suffix** is added to the end of a word to change its meaning.

    harm   harm*less*

The part of the word that a suffix is added to is called a **root word.**

    *help*ful   *exhibit*or

Suffix	Meaning	Example
al	like, referring to	coast*al*
able, ible	able to be	break*able*, flex*ible*
er, or	one who	sing*er*, sail*or*
ful	full of	help*ful*
less	without	hope*less*
y	what kind	snow*y*
ly	how	quick*ly*
ist	one who does	art*ist*
ness	quality of being	kind*ness*
ish	like, somewhat	yellow*ish*

▶ **Directions** Complete the table by adding a suffix to the word. The new word should have the meaning listed in the second column. Use the list above to help you.

Word + Suffix	Meaning
1. nervous_____	quality of being nervous
2. accept_____	can be accepted
3. fear_____	without fear
4. child_____	like a child
5. cartoon_____	one who creates cartoons

▶ **Directions** Read each sentence. Add the suffix that makes the most sense when added to the word. Use the list above to help you.

6. The project wasn't working; the whole thing felt hope_____.

7. We had to drive slow_____ on the ice-covered roads.

8. Carlos is the fastest walk_____ I know.

9. I'm sure John can do it himself; it's a manage_____ task.

10. The flowers have a green_____ tint to them.

11. The tire_____ attendant worked through the entire evening.

Name _____ Date _____

Using a Pronunciation Guide

An important part of most dictionaries is the **pronunciation guide.** This helps the reader to know how to say new words. Each word has a pronunciation next to it with symbols that show how to sound out the word. This is called a *phonetic spelling.* The guide explains what the symbols mean. It also gives a familiar word in which the sound is heard.

The words in the dictionary are also divided into **syllables.** Syllables are parts of words that have only one vowel sound. The syllable that is pronounced most strongly will have an **accent mark (').**

a	add	i	it	o͝o	took	oi	oil
ā	ace	ī	ice	o͞o	pool	ou	pout
â	care	o	odd	u	up	ng	ring
ä	palm	ō	open	û	burn	th	thin
e	end	ô	order	yo͞o	fuse	th	this
ē	equal					zh	vision

ə = { a in *above* e in *sicken* i in *possible*
      o in *melon* u in *circus* }

HBJ School Dictionary

▶ **Directions** Use the pronunciation key above to write the word shown in each dictionary respelling. Then use each word in a sentence. Use a dictionary for help with definitions.

1. (ret′ nə) _____

2. (op′ ti kəl) _____

3. (ri flek′ shən) _____

4. (ī′ sīt) _____

5. (pyo͞o′ pəl) _____

6. (ôr′ gən) _____

▶ **Directions** Find each word in a dictionary. Write the word, placing a hyphen between syllables.

7. concave _____   10. farsighted _____

8. convex _____   11. cornea _____

9. nearsighted _____   12. recognize _____

Words with Multiple Meanings

A **homograph** is a word with the same spelling as another word but with a different meaning and origin and, sometimes, a different pronunciation. Homographs might be listed under one entry word, or as separate entry words.

▶ **Directions** Read the meaning(s) of each word. Then write a sentence for each of the meanings shown.

bow¹ (bou) *v.* to bend down one's head or bend one's body in respect, agreement, worship, recognition, etc.

bow² (bō) *n.* a curve, bend.

bow³ (bou) *n.* the front part of a ship or boat.

down¹ (doun) *adv.* from a higher to a lower place. *adj.* in a lower place; on the ground.

down² (doun) *n.* soft, fluffy feathers, as the outer covering on young birds or an inner layer of feathers on adult birds.

down³ (doun) *n.* an expanse of open, high, grassy land: *usually used in plural.*

cold (kōld) *adj.* of a temperature significantly or noticeably lower than average, normal, expected, or comfortable. *n.* a contagious, viral infection of the respiratory passages, especially of the nose and throat.

1. down¹ _____
2. down² _____
3. bow¹ _____
4. bow² _____
5. bow³ _____
6. cold (adjective) _____
7. cold (noun) _____

▶ **Directions** On another sheet of paper, draw pictures to show two meanings for each of the words below. Use a dictionary for help with definitions.

coat   fall   float   pine   point   row

Name _____ Date _____

Using Guide Words and Entry Words

The words in a dictionary are listed in alphabetical order. Each page of a dictionary has **guide words** at the top. Guide words are also in alphabetical order. They are the first and last words on the page. The word on the left is the first word on the page, and the word on the right is the last word on the page. Look at the example below.

Entry words are the words that are defined in the dictionary. Every entry word on a page will fall in alphabetical order between the guide words.

---

duplicate   Dutch

du pli cate (v. d(y)o͞o′ plə kāt, n., adj. d(y)o͞o′ plə kit) v. **du pli cat ed, du pli cat ing,** n., adj. 1. v. to copy exactly or do again. That work of art could not be *duplicated*. 2. n. an exact copy: a *duplicate* of a letter. 3. adj. made like or exactly corresponding to something else: a *duplicate* key. 4. adj. in pairs; double.
du ra ble (d(y)o͝or′ ə bəl) adj. lasting a long time without wearing out: a *durable* material. —**dur′ a ble ness** n. —**dur′ a bly** adv.
du ra tion (d(y)o͞o rā′ shən) n. the time during which anything goes on or lasts: the *duration* of the winter.

▶ **Directions** Use the sample dictionary page above to answer these questions.

1. What are the guide words on this page? _____

2. What would the last word on this page be? _____

3. Would the word *during* appear on this page? _____

   Why or why not? _____

4. Which entry word means "an exact copy"? _____

5. How many entry words are shown in the sample? _____

6. How many meanings for the word *duplicate* are shown? _____

7. What is meaning 3 of *duplicate*? _____

8. Write a sentence using the word *duration*. _____

_____

Name _____ Date _____

Using a Dictionary

▶ **Directions** Look at the sample dictionary page below. Use the sample to answer the questions and to follow the directions.

---

quaint   **quill**

quaint (kwānt) *adj.* unusual or odd.
quan ti ty (kwăn′ tĭ tē) *n.* a number or an amount.
quar rel (kwŏr′ ĕl) 1. *n.* an angry fight. 2. *v.* to find fault.
quar ry[1] (kwôr′ ē) (kwär′ ē) *n.* a square or diamond-shaped piece of glass, tile, etc.
quar ry[2] (kwôr′ ē) (kwär′ ē) *n.* something that is hunted; prey.
quar ry[3] (kwôr′ ē) (kwär′ ē) *n.* place from which to get stone.
queen (kwēn) *n.* 1. a female ruler; the wife of a king. 2. a playing card with the picture of a queen.
question (kwĕs′ chŭn) 1. *n.* something that is asked. 2. *v.* to ask.
quick (kwĭk) *adj.* fast.
quill (kwĭl) *n.* 1. a feather. 2. a kind of writing pen.

---

1. What are the guide words on this page? _____

2. How many entry words are shown in this sample? _____

3. What part of speech is *quarrel* when it means "an angry fight"? _____

4. How many syllables are in the word *quantity*? _____

5. How many syllables are in the word *question*? _____

6. Write two sentences, each using a different meaning for the word *queen*.
   _____
   _____

7. What adjective has the same vowel sound as the *a* in *face*? _____

8. Could the word *quilt* be on this page? _____ Tell why or why not. _____
   _____

9. Which word has two different pronunciations? _____

10. Which word is a homograph? _____

11. Use one of the entry words from this page and create your own sentence.
    _____
    _____

Name _____   Date _____

Show What You Know

▶ **Directions** Read the paragraph about clouds. Find each word in dark print in the dictionary. Write the meanings that make sense in the paragraph on the lines beside the words.

Cloud Cover

Clouds are one of the most **obvious,** and **spectacular,** features of weather. Clouds can take several forms. They can be thin and wispy, or **dense** and **billowy.** How do clouds form? Water rises from Earth's surface to become water **vapor** in the air. You cannot see the vapor because it is a gas. As the water vapor **expands,** it begins to cool. The water vapor **condenses** around tiny things in the air, such as dust or smoke. It forms **droplets.** The droplets can be seen as clouds. Clouds form in different shapes. Their shapes depend on their height, the temperature of the air, and the amount of water vapor in the air.

1. obvious _____
2. spectacular _____
3. dense _____
4. billowy _____
5. vapor _____
6. expands _____
7. condenses _____
8. droplets _____

▶ **Directions** Answer each question.

9. How did the dictionary help you to understand the paragraph about clouds?
_____

10. Do you think it is helpful to use a dictionary while you are reading? Tell why or why not.
_____
_____

Unit 2 Resources

Name _____ Date _____

News Article Diagram

Greenville Teacher Wins Outstanding Teacher Award ← 1.

2. → **Jay Beard**
Staff Writer

3. → GREENVILLE Tuesday, May 20, 2008 – James Johnson Elementary teacher Suzanne Cook won the Outstanding Teacher Award from the National Elementary School Teacher's Association (NESTA). The $5,000 prize was presented by NESTA's president, Dr. Marcus Mosby, at the group's Annual Awards Banquet last Saturday evening at the Greenville Manor Hotel. Cook, a fifth grade teacher, was one of five finalists from across the nation. — 4.

Each finalist submitted a videotape of himself or herself teaching one lesson. "Mrs. Cook's innovative and enthusiastic teaching style made her the

5. → clear winner," Dr. Mosby said. — 6.

The James Johnson Elementary School hosted a celebration for Cook Monday morning. Food was provided by Rosie's Kitchen, and the Greenville orchestra entertained the crowd.

When asked about the award, Cook said, "Being recognized for something that I love to do is a great honor. But seeing my students' faces when they truly understand a new concept is the real award that I get to experience every day." — 7.

1. _____   5. _____
2. _____   6. _____
3. _____   7. _____
4. _____

Name _____   Date _____

Understanding a News Article

Newspapers are a type of resource people use to find up-to-date information. Newspapers are divided into different sections and feature **news articles**. News articles tell facts about recent events. The **reporter**, or person who authored the news article, wants to answer *Who? What? When? Where? Why?* and *How?* within the article.

News articles include specific parts to help the reader.
- The **headline** is the words printed in larger type above the news article. The headline captures the reader's attention and tells the main idea of the article.
- The **dateline** is always found at the beginning of the news article. It tells when and where the article was written.
- The **lead paragraph,** or introduction, gives the most important facts.
- The **supporting details** give more information about the event. These middle paragraphs support the lead paragraph.
- The **conclusion** presents the final details of the article.
- A **quotation,** or quote, is the exact words that a speaker says. A quotation must always include quotation marks (" ") before and after the speaker's exact words. Quotation marks are not used when the exact words of the speaker are not written.

▶ **Directions** Use the news article on page 18 to answer the questions.

1. What is the main idea of the article? _____

2. Who received an award? _____

3. What is the name of the award that was presented? _____

4. When was the award presented? _____

5. Who presented the award? _____

6. Give two additional details from the article. _____
   _____

7. Where was Mrs. Cook given the award? _____

8. Why was Mrs. Cook given the award? _____

▶ **Directions** Look at the news article diagram on page 18. Use the words below to label the diagram.

| conclusion | dateline | headline | lead paragraph |
| quotation | reporter | supporting details | |

Name _____ Date _____

Using a News Article

Southwest Little League Advances to Sectionals

Staff Writer

SMITHTOWN July 31, 2008 – The Southwest Smithtown Little League 10–11-year-old Tigers team won the North Carolina District Nine tournament last Monday night against Duncan Little League, 10–7. The team advances to the North Carolina Sectional Tournament this weekend in Raleigh.

"It's great to see the kids so proud of their hard work," said Team Manager Scott Frank of the win.

The team originally lost their first game of the season 2–0 to Duncan. They then went on to win their next five games by a combined score of 63–17. "I think our boys did an excellent job working together as a team," Frank said. "That, to me, is what sets our boys apart."

Team members come from all parts of West and Southwest Smithtown, with several students from Peak and Highland Park Elementary Schools and from Westlake and Miles Middle Schools.

▶ **Directions** Use the news article above to answer the questions.

1. Who won the tournament? _____

2. What was the name of the tournament? _____

3. When did the tournament take place? _____

4. Who is the team manager for the Tigers team? _____

5. What is a school attended by several team members? _____

6. Write down one of the quotes from the article. _____

   _____

7. What is the article's headline? _____

8. In what section of the newspaper might you find this news article? _____

9. Is this article fiction or nonfiction? _____ Explain your answer.

   _____

   _____

10. Who wrote the article? _____

Name _____   Date _____

Show What You Know

▶ **Directions** Find an article in a newspaper. Use the article you found to answer the questions and to follow the directions.

1. What is the headline of the article? _____

2. What is the dateline of the article? _____

3. What is the main subject of the article?
   _____
   _____

4. If there are any quotations, list two of them.
   _____
   _____

5. List six facts or details from the article.
   _____
   _____
   _____
   _____
   _____
   _____

▶ **Directions** Work with a partner to create your own news article about an important event that has recently happened. Use the newspaper for topics to write about. Be sure to include a title, a headline, a lead paragraph, supporting details, and a quotation.

_____
_____
_____
_____
_____

Name _____ Date _____

Brochure Diagram

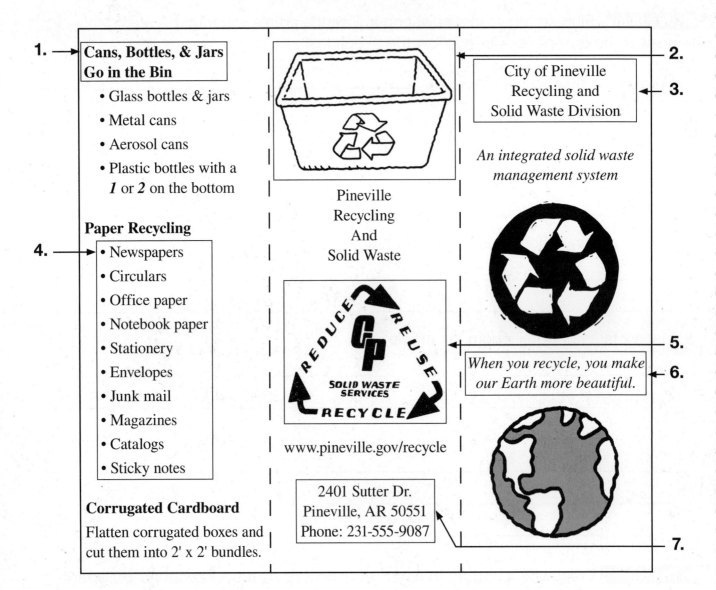

1. _____
2. _____
3. _____
4. _____
5. _____
6. _____
7. _____

Name _____ Date _____

Understanding a Brochure

Brochures can be a good starting point for gathering information about an organization, location, or product. A brochure is a small, unbound, printed booklet or pamphlet designed to inform, educate, or persuade. Good brochures present the most significant or most interesting details in a clear and organized format.

Key information in a brochure can include the following information.

- **name** of location, business, or organization that has published the brochure
- **contact information** that includes the name of organization, address, phone number, and an e-mail or Web page address
- **headline** that creates curiosity, states a benefit, or otherwise entices the reader to open the brochure and read more; or that states the name of the product, project, or described process
- **logo** that is a symbol or graphic that represents a particular company or organization
- **slogan** that is a phrase or motto used by a business, a group, or an individual to express a goal or belief
- **graphic** or artistic images that support the text in the brochure and make the brochure more exciting to read
- **headings** that are usually in dark print that divide the brochure into different sections by a subject or category
- **photos** of products, places, or people
- **text** in short, easy-to-read blocks; many times the text includes bullets

▶ **Directions** Look at the brochure diagram on page 22. Use the words below to label the diagram.

contact information	graphic	heading	logo
name of organization	slogan	text	

Name _____ Date _____

Using a Brochure

▶ **Directions** Use the brochure on page 22 to answer each question and to follow the directions.

1. What is the organization's Web address?
   _____

2. What are the three different main types of recycling?
   _____

3. List three items that can go in the bin.
   _____

4. What must you do to recycle corrugated cardboard?
   _____

5. List three recyclable paper items.
   _____

6. Describe how each of the three graphic images supports the messages presented in the brochure.
   _____
   _____
   _____

7. How can you find out which day to set out your recyclable trash?
   _____

8. How would you dispose of a bottle that has a *3* or a *4* on the bottom?
   _____

9. Who most likely paid to design and print the brochure?
   _____

10. How does the front of the brochure capture the reader's attention?
    _____

Show What You Know

▶ **Directions** Take a separate sheet of paper and fold it lengthwise into three equal parts.

You will design a brochure on the front of the three sections of paper. Use page 22 as an example of the layout.

Your brochure should be about one of your favorite places. For example, you might choose a favorite library, restaurant, or theme park. Remember to have a goal for the brochure (to inform, educate, or persuade). Include the following elements in your brochure.

- Name of your favorite place
- Contact information
- Two graphics
- Slogan
- Two headings
- At least three bulleted details under each heading

Name _____   Date _____

Almanac Diagram

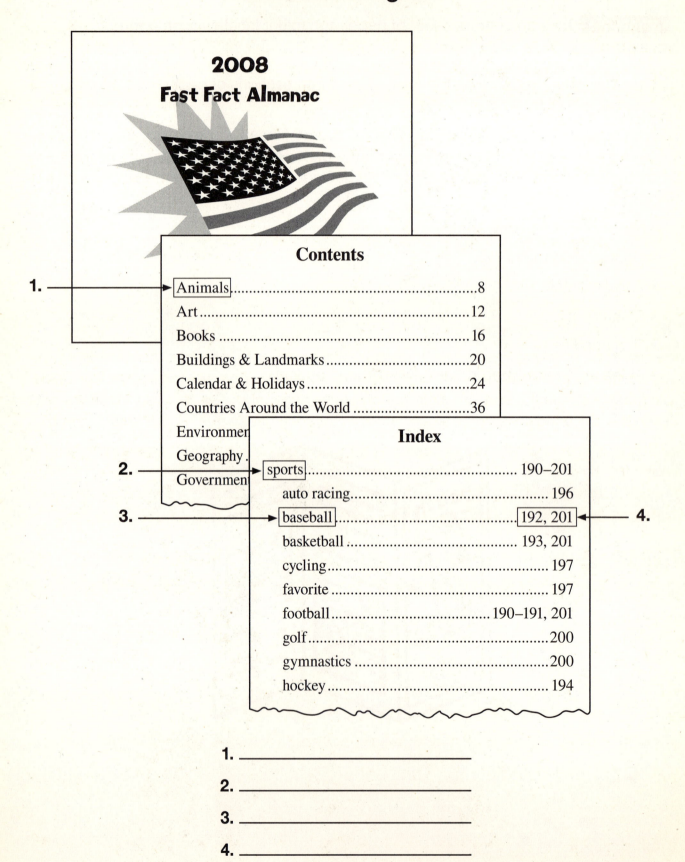

1. _____
2. _____
3. _____
4. _____

Name _____   Date _____

Understanding an Almanac

An **almanac** is a reference book that is updated and published once a year. It is a valuable research tool that provides information on a variety of topics including *people, countries, animals,* the *environment,* and *history.* An almanac can be used to find facts quickly.

Almanacs, like other books, have two main organizational features—a table of contents and an index.

- The **table of contents** is in the front of the almanac. **Topic categories** and the page numbers where they can be found are listed here. The table of contents gives you a general idea of what material is covered within the almanac.

- The **index** is in the back of the almanac. The index is a complete listing of the main **topics** and **subtopics** in the almanac. The topics are listed in alphabetical order. If there is more detailed information on the subject, you will find a subtopic listed under the topic. The index is the best place to start when you are looking for a specific fact in the almanac.

Before you can search for information in the index, you will need to determine what the keywords are in the information for which you are searching. Looking up the keywords will most likely be the best place to find the information. For example, suppose you were given the following research question: *"What is the largest planet in our solar system?"*

In this example, the keywords are *planet* and *solar system.* Now you can search the index for the *planet* and *solar system* topics to find the answer to your research topic. You will most likely find your answer in one or both places. If you are looking up a person's name, you must look under the last name.

▶ **Directions** Use the words below to label the parts of the almanac on page 26.

| page numbers | subtopic | topic | topic category |

Name _____   Date _____

Using an Almanac

TEXAS
Origin of Name: From a Native American word meaning "friends"
State Abbreviation: TX
Residents: Texans
Entered Union (rank): December 29, 1845 (28)
Ratification of Constitution: 1876
Capital: Austin
Song: "Texas, Our Texas"
Motto: Friendship
Flower: Bluebonnet
Bird: Mockingbird
Tree: Pecan
Plant: Prickly Pear Cactus
Reptile: Horned Lizard
Mammal: Longhorn
Small Mammal: Armadillo
Flying Mammal: Mexican Free-Tailed Bat
Stone: Petrified Palmwood
Fish: Guadalupe Bass
Seashell: Lightning Whelk
Folk Dance: Square Dance
Dish: Chili
Fruit: Texas Red Grapefruit
Gem: Texas Blue Topaz
Gemstone Cut: Lone Star Cut
Grass: Sideoats Grama
Nickname: Lone Star State
Population: (2006): 23,507,783
Largest Cities (by population): Houston, San Antonio, Dallas, Austin, Ft. Worth
Largest County (by population): Harris County
Bordering States: Arkansas, Louisiana, New Mexico, Oklahoma
Land Area: 261,797 sq mi (678,054 sq km)
Time Zone: Central Standard Time
State Forests: 5 (7,314 acres)
State Parks: 115 (+600,000 acres)
Flags Flown Over State: Spain (1519–1685; 1690–1821); France (1685–1690); Mexico (1821–1836); Republic of Texas (1836–1845); Confederate States of America (1861–1865); United States of America (1845–1861; 1865–present)

▶ **Directions** Use the almanac page above to answer the questions.

1. In what category from an almanac's table of contents do you think this topic belongs?
_____

2. When did Texas become part of the United States? _____

3. What was the population of Texas in 2006? _____

4. What is the Texas state flower? _____

5. What is the third-largest city in Texas? _____

6. What is the capital of Texas? _____

7. How many flags have flown over Texas? _____

8. How many states border Texas? _____

9. What does the word *Texas* originate from? _____
_____

Name _____ Date _____

Show What You Know

▶ **Directions** Use an almanac to answer the questions.

1. What does the flag of Algeria look like? _____

2. In Greek mythology, who was the Greek goddess of love and of beauty?
   _____

3. What was the population of the United States in the most recent year it was recorded?
   _____

4. For what is Bill Gates famous? _____

5. What year did the Bill of Rights go into effect? _____

6. Who was the 10th president of the United States? _____

7. What are the seven continents? _____
   _____
   _____

▶ **Directions** Write two questions for which answers can be found in the almanac. Trade questions with a classmate and use the almanac to answer each other's questions. Check to see that your partner answered your questions correctly.

Question 1: _____
_____

Answer: _____
_____

Question 2: _____
_____

Answer: _____
_____

Name _____   Date _____

Advertisement Diagram

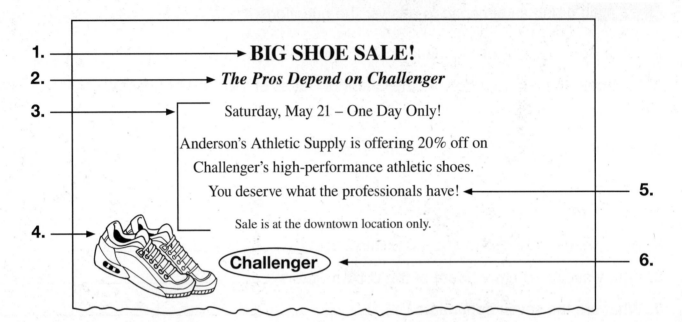

1. _____
2. _____
3. _____
4. _____
5. _____
6. _____

Name _____   Date _____

Understanding an Advertisement

Mass media are used to get information to large numbers of people. Newspapers, magazines, and television are examples of mass media.

Advertising is a large part of many types of mass media. Organizations pay to place **advertisements (ads)** in the mass media so that they can be seen by large audiences.

Print Advertisements are a type of ad used in newspapers and magazines. The following components are part of print ads.

- **Headline** Headlines are generally presented in large, boldfaced print at the top of a print ad. They are designed to grab the attention of the reader. Common headlines might tell people how they can make money, save money, or benefit from using a particular product or service.
- **Body** The body expands on the main idea that is presented in the headline. In the body, additional facts are listed, and detailed descriptions are provided. Limitations or exclusions to a special are also found in the body text.
- **Photographs** and **Illustrations** Print ads usually include visual images that will help the reader remember the ad.
- **Slogan** A slogan is often used to summarize the advantages or strengths of the product or service in the ad.
- **Logo** The logo is a distinctive company image or graphic. The logo provides another visual image to help the reader recognize the business or organization that paid for the ad.

When reviewing advertisements, it is important to remember that the people who make ads use **persuasive tactics,** or ways to get people to buy their products. Some persuasive tactics include the following.
- **Bandwagon** Everyone else is doing it; you should too.
- **Celebrity** A celebrity likes the product; you will too.
- **Before and After** Use the product, and you will notice a big change!
- **Flattery** You are great! You deserve this product.

▶ **Directions** Look at the advertisement diagram on page 30. Use the words below to label the diagram.

| body | headline | illustration | logo | persuasive tactic | slogan |

Name _____   Date _____

Using an Advertisement

> **Introducing the New and Improved RoboGirl Plus!**
>
> *RoboGirl Plus! Caters to Your Every Need!*
>
> Now is your chance to own the latest advancement in technology. You'll notice big improvements in your quality of life with this purchase! *RoboGirl Plus!* will do everything you don't have time to do and the things you don't want to do—taking out the garbage, cleaning your house, washing your clothes, running errands. You work hard; you deserve *RoboGirl Plus!*
>
> *Introductory price of $999.99.
>
> Visit www.robogirl.us for more information and to see a product demo.
>
> **Robo Industries**   *Price valid for first month of product release. See company Web site for complete details.

▶ **Directions** Use the ad to answer the following questions and to follow the directions.

1. What type of product or service is being advertised? _____

2. Which persuasive tactics are used in the ad? _____

3. What section of the newspaper might you find this ad in? _____

4. Who do you think paid for the ad? _____

5. What is the ad trying to make you believe? _____
   _____

6. Why is it important to read the entire ad, including the fine, or smaller, print?
   _____

7. Write an additional slogan for the ad using the following persuasive tactics.

   Bandwagon: _____
   _____

   Celebrity: _____
   _____

Name _____ Date _____

Show What You Know

▶ **Directions** Use an advertisement from a newspaper or magazine to answer the following questions.

1. What is the headline of the ad? _____

2. Is there a logo in the ad? If so, describe it. _____
_____

3. Are any persuasive tactics used in the ad? If so, what?
_____
_____

4. Are photos or illustrations used in the ad? If so, describe them.
_____
_____

5. Would you buy the product or use the services? Why or why not? _____
_____

6. For what kind of audience do you think this ad is intended?
_____

7. Do you like the ad? Why or why not? _____
_____

▶ **Directions** Working with a partner, discuss ideas for a print advertisement. Then design an ad on another sheet of paper. Include the following elements in your ad: headline, body, illustration, slogan, logo, and two persuasive tactics. When you have completed your ad, use the space below to describe the elements included in the ad. Be sure to provide specific information and tell how each of the elements works to persuade the audience.

_____
_____
_____
_____
_____

Name _____ Date _____

Web Site Diagram

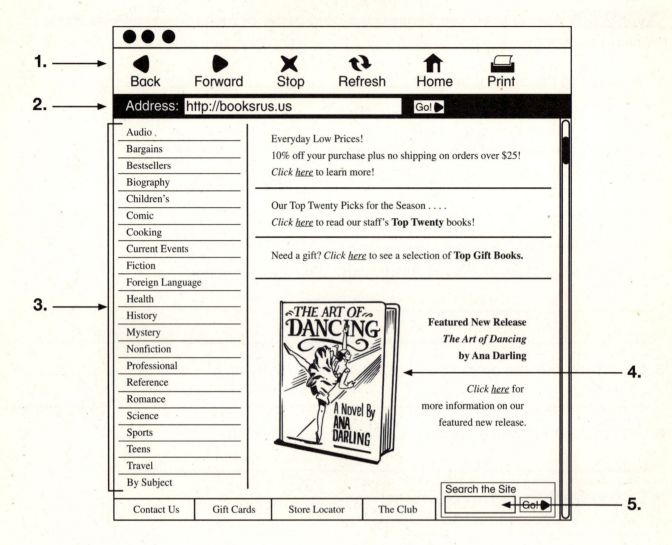

1. _____
2. _____
3. _____
4. _____
5. _____

Name _____ Date _____

Understanding a Web Site

A **Web site** is an electronic document written in a computer language called **HTML** (Hypertext Markup Language). A Web site consists of one or more pages that relate to a common theme. The theme may be a person, business, organization, or subject, such as sports. Each page has a unique address known as an **URL** (Uniform Resource Locator), which identifies its location. A user might visit a Web site to learn new information, to buy a product, to play games, or to communicate with others. It is important to remember that the information presented on a Web site may not always be accurate, so you should always use another source to ensure it is good information.

- The first page of a Web site is called the **home page.** The home page is like a table of contents for the information on the site. Web pages usually contain **hyperlinks,** or links to other Web pages. The pages also contain elements to make them more interesting. Such elements include **graphics,** video, animation, and sound.

- A user can move from page to page within a Web site by clicking on links. A user can also use different tools, such as the back and forward buttons, to navigate around a site.

  ◀ Back   ▶ Forward   ↻ Refresh

- The first page of a Web site usually includes a lot of information. But sometimes it may not show exactly what a user is looking for. In instances such as this, a user can often use the site's **Search** feature. A user can type in what he or she is looking for, and a list of related topics will appear.

▶ **Directions** Use the Web site on page 34 to answer each question.

1. What type of business is shown on the Web site? _____
2. What link would a user click on to find a location of a store? _____
3. What is the Web site's URL? _____
4. What might be a user's reason for visiting this Web site? _____
5. What does a user receive if he or she spends over $25? _____
6. Does this Web site have a search feature? _____

▶ **Directions** Look at the Web site diagram on page 34. Use the words below to label the diagram.

| graphic | hyperlinks | search | tools | URL |

Using a Web Site

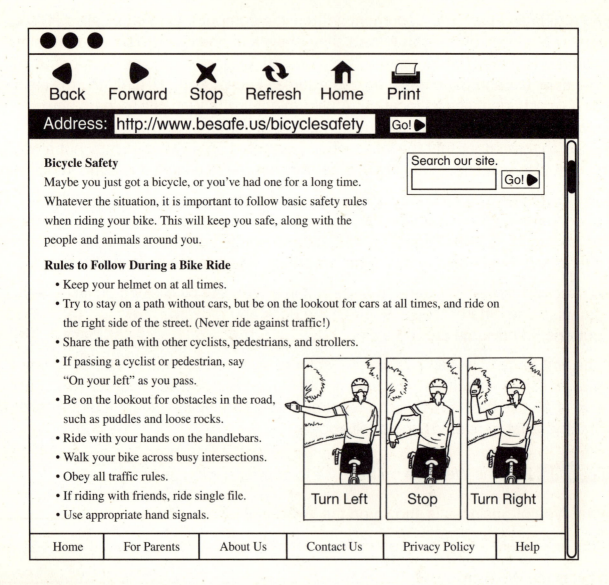

▶ **Directions** Use the Web site to answer each question and to follow the directions.

1. Who might visit this Web page? _____

2. What is the URL for this Web page? _____

3. What link would you click on to learn more information about the business that owns the Web site? _____

4. Does this Web page include graphics? If so, describe one. _____

5. What link would you click on to go to the site's home page? _____

6. What other type of information might you find on this Web site? _____

Name _____ Date _____

Show What You Know

▶ **Directions** Visit two Web sites listed below. Note all the parts of a Web site that each has. Complete the Venn diagram, comparing and contrasting the Web sites.

http://www.ri.gov/kids/
(Rhode Island)

http://www.secretary.state.nc.us/kidspg/
(North Carolina)

http://www.state.de.us/gic/kidspage/
(Delaware)

http://www.state.ak.us/local/kids/home.html
(Arkansas)

http://www.state.nj.us/hangout_nj/
(New Jersey)

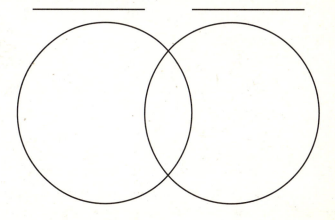

▶ **Directions** Select one of the Web sites you did not visit above. Write five questions you would like to learn about this state from the Web site. Visit the Web site and answer your questions.

Question 1: _____

Answer: _____

Question 2: _____

Answer: _____

Question 3: _____

Answer: _____

Question 4: _____

Answer: _____

Question 5: _____

Answer: _____

Unit 3
Text Features

Understanding a Title Page/Copyright Page

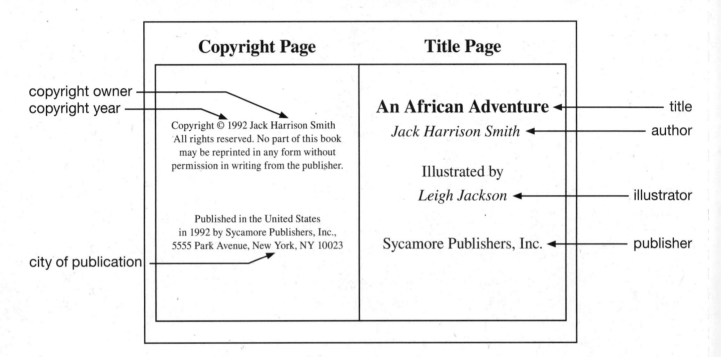

The **title page** is placed at the beginning of a book. It usually tells the title of the book and the names of the **author** and **publisher.** The author is the person that wrote the book. Some publications have more than one author. The company that puts the book together is the publisher. If the book has drawings, the name of the **illustrator** will also be on the title page.

A **copyright** is a set of exclusive legal rights that gives an owner the right to produce, publish, or sell any part of a book, song, etc. The **copyright page** of a book is typically found on the back of the title page, but may sometimes be placed to the left of the title page. The copyright page includes the **copyright date,** or year the book is published, and the name of the **copyright owner.** The copyright owner is usually the author, but may be an organization or corporation, such as the publisher. The copyright page also includes the **city of publication,** or the city where the material was published.

▶ **Directions** On another sheet of paper, write five true and false sentences about title and copyright pages. Trade your sentences with a partner and check to see if your partner chooses *True* or *False* correctly for each statement.

Name _____   Date _____

Using a Title Page/Copyright Page

> **Directions** Use the title and copyright pages on page 38 to answer the questions below.

1. What is the title of the book? _____

2. Who is the author of the book? _____

3. Who published the book? _____

4. In what city was the book published? _____

5. In what year was the book published? _____

6. Does the book contain drawings? How do you know? _____
_____
_____

7. Who is the copyright owner? _____

8. Who might like this book? _____

9. Who would you have to contact to receive permission to copy the book?
_____

10. Does the title page give you enough information to know whether the book is fiction or nonfiction? Explain your answer.
_____
_____
_____

Name _____ Date _____

Show What You Know

▶ **Directions** Choose a book from your classroom or library and find the title and copyright pages. Use the pages to answer the questions below.

1. What is the title of the book? _____
2. When was the book published? _____
3. Who might like this book? _____
4. When was the book published? _____
5. What is the name of the publishing firm? _____
6. In what city was the book published? _____
7. Is the book illustrated? If so, who is the illustrator? _____
8. Who is the copyright owner of the book? _____
9. Who is the author of the book? _____
10. Is someone able to copy this book without permission? Tell why or why not.
    _____
11. In your own words, what is a title page? _____
    _____
12. In your own words, what does *copyright* mean? _____
    _____
13. How might these two pages be helpful to you when you are conducting a research project?
    _____
    _____

Name _____ Date _____

Understanding a Table of Contents

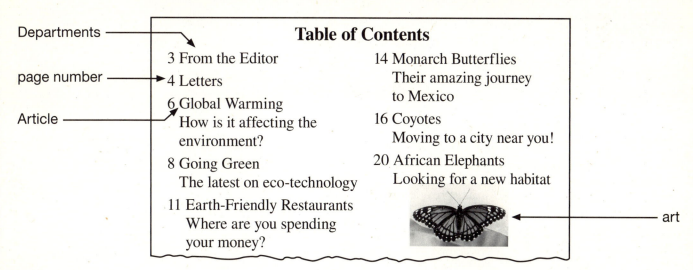

The **table of contents** is an important feature of a publication, such as a book or magazine. Skimming the information in the table of contents helps the reader become familiar with the organization of the magazine and its contents.

A magazine's table of contents usually includes a list of all of the articles, stories, and features in the order that they appear in the magazine; the **page number** on which the articles, stories, or features can be found; and **photos with captions** that relate to some of the articles.

Many magazines contain sections that appear in every issue of the publication. In the table of contents, these sections and their page numbers are listed under *Departments*. For example, a letter from the chief editor of the magazine is featured in every issue of some magazines.

Many books contain chapters or units. The table of contents is organized in order of these chapters or units and lists the chapter and unit names.

▶ **Directions** Use the table of contents diagram above to answer each question.

1. What type of magazine is this table of contents most likely from?

_____

2. What is the name of the article that begins on page 20? _____

3. What is the longest article shown in the table of contents? _____

4. Which article is about migration? _____

5. On what page would you find a letter from the editor? _____

Name _____ Date _____

Using a Table of Contents

▶ **Directions** Use the table of contents below to answer each question.

Table of Contents

14 Leadership in Washington
More women in positions
of power

16 The Race for the Presidency
Who will be the next
U.S. leader?

20 Education Nation
Schools in the South: Feeling
the pressure to perform

22 A Look at the Big Screen
It's award time! A look at this
year's favorite movies

26 Soccer to 'Em
Will the Kicks be the next
world champs?

28 Art in the City
A look at Chicago's growing
art scene

30 Looking at Health
How do Americans measure up?

34 A Look at Rural America
How are America's crops
surviving the drought?

Departments:
Letter from the Editor 4
Top News Stories 5
A Look at Technology 10

---

1. What is most likely the title of this magazine? Circle your answer.

   Science for Kids   BeautySplurge   *News Now*

2. In which article would you be most likely to read about museums?
_____

3. Which sections can be found in each publication of this magazine?
_____

4. On which page could you read about farming? _____

5. On which pages will you most likely find the most current news stories? _____

6. How many pages long is the article "Leadership in Washington"? _____

Name _____ Date _____

Show What You Know

▶ **Directions** You have been asked to write a magazine for your school. The magazine will communicate current and upcoming school happenings, stories, and information.

1. Brainstorm the most important information that should be included in the magazine. You might include classroom highlights for each grade level, important dates to remember, and a letter from the principal.
2. Interview teachers and staff to help you decide what information should be included in the magazine.
3. Use the space below to create a table of contents for your magazine. You should include at least seven articles with a title and page number for each article. Give your magazine a name.

Magazine Name: _____

Name _____ Date _____

Understanding Headings and Captions

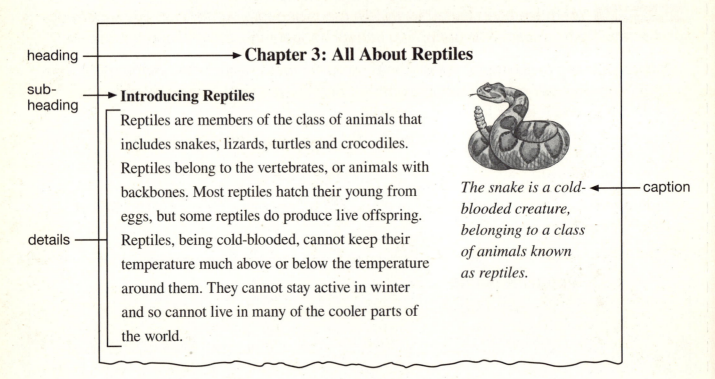

When a reader looks at an article, he or she can *skim* the information to get an idea what it is about. This means quickly looking over the words in the article to get an overview of its contents. When a reader uses a text to answer questions or to find information, he or she can *scan,* or examine, the text to find more specific information.

Looking at **headings** and **captions** is a good way to search for specific information that is covered in the article. Headings generally tell what the article is about. The **subheading** tells what the paragraph that follows the subheading is about. **Details** are given in the sentences under the subheading. The captions are words or sentences under a picture or diagram that tell more about it. The information in a caption might not be included anywhere else in the text, so it is always important for the reader to look at the caption.

▶ **Directions** Write a new heading and subheading for the paragraph above on reptiles. Also write a new caption for the picture.

Heading: _____ Subheading: _____

Caption: _____

Using Headings and Captions

▶ **Directions** Read the information below. Fill in the heading and/or subheading blank lines for each paragraph. Then write a caption for each picture.

**Chapter 4:
Police**

Police are community helpers who keep us safe on the streets and in our homes. Every country in the world has a police system. Each level of government, from the village or city level to the national level, often has a police force. These forces work together to enforce laws, prevent crime, and protect lives and property.

1. Heading: _____

2. Subheading: _____

Most police departments have three main duties: (1) general policing carried out by uniformed patrol officers; (2) detective work; and (3) traffic control. Patrol officers may travel their routes on foot, in squad cars, or on motorcycles. They are prepared to handle accidents, crimes, or disturbances of any sort. Detectives investigate special kinds of crimes. Detectives usually wear ordinary street clothes so that they will not be recognized as police officers. That is why detectives are sometimes called plainclothes officers. Traffic officers have special duties that include directing traffic; enforcing parking, speed, and other traffic safety laws; and inspecting vehicles to make sure that they meet various safety and licensing requirements.

3. Caption: _____

4. Heading: _____

Texas had the first state police system in the United States. The Texas Rangers, organized in 1835, at first served as a border patrol. They later took over general police work. In the late 1800s, police officers were called constables. The name *cop,* a slang term for a police officer, may have come from the initials *C.O.P.,* which stood for *Constable on Patrol.* However, some authorities claim that *cop* is a shortened form of *copper,* a name that referred to the star-shaped copper badges police officers wore.

5. Caption: _____

Name _____ Date _____

Show What You Know

▶ **Directions** Using a magazine, choose an article that includes a heading, subheading, illustration, and caption. Scan the text to find the keywords and details of the article. Complete the chart below:

Heading	
Subheading	
Caption	
Keywords/Details	
Write 4 to 5 sentences summarizing the article based on the heading, subheading, caption, and the keywords and details you found.	

▶ **Directions** Now read the article to answer the questions below and to follow the directions.

1. How does the heading help you know what the article is about?

   _____

2. How do the illustration and caption support or help explain the main idea of the article?

   _____

3. Write a different heading and subheading to replace the ones in the article.

   Heading: _____

   Subheading: _____

4. Describe a different illustration and caption that would apply to the article.

   Illustration: _____

   Caption: _____

Name _____   Date _____

Understanding an Index

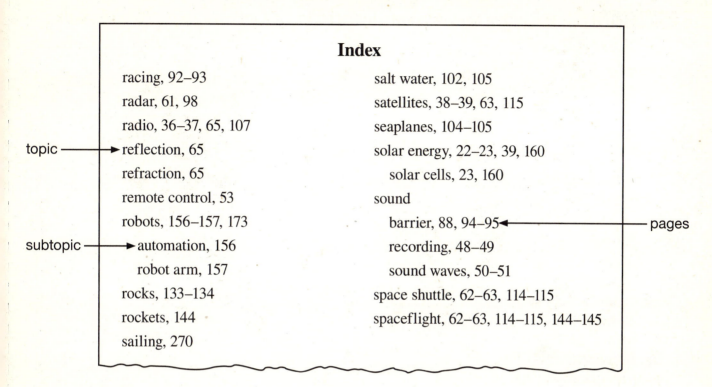

The **index** is found in the back of a book. It lists many topics from the book and the pages where topics can be found. Sometimes there is a **topic** that has **subtopics,** or more detailed topics, about it. For instance, if the topic in the index is *sports,* some subtopics might be *basketball, football, golf,* and *soccer.* An index is used to find the **page numbers** that have information about a topic.

▶ **Directions** Use the index above to answer each question.

1. In what order are the topics arranged in the index? _____

2. On what pages can you learn about rocks? _____

3. What three topics can be found on page 65? _____
_____

4. How many pages have information about solar energy? _____

5. What can you learn about on pages 61 and 98? _____

6. On what pages might you find out what year the sound barrier was first broken?
_____

Name _____ Date _____

Using an Index

▶ **Directions** Use the index to answer each question.

Index

A
American Indians, 108–109
  Cherokee, 70–71
  Delaware, 203–204
  history of, 203–205
  legends, 208, 209 (picture), 210–211
  Navajo, 204
  Osage, 205
  Wampanoag, 222
American Revolution, 234
  causes, 232
  events, 233–234
  people, 232–239
Artifacts, 129, 199, 206 (picture), 207, 216, 233, 237, 248, 271, 305, 321, 324

B
Bell, Alexander Graham, 259 (picture)

Boston, Massachusetts, 231 (map)
Boston Tea Party, 232
Branches of Government, 308, 309 (graph)

C
Carter, Jimmy, 313
Carver, George Washington, 166 (picture)
Chávez, Cesar, 138, 139 (picture)
Citizens, 282
  elections, 299–301
  government, 283, 299–301
  laws, 293 (picture)
  rights of, 10–11, 283
  voting, 301
Colonies, 219 (map), 230, 231 (map)
  American Revolution, 234

Declaration of Independence, 233
Jamestown, 219 (map), 220–221
Plymouth, 219 (map), 222–223
Columbus, Christopher, 214, 215 (map)
Communities, 28
Constitution of the United States, 306–307
  branches of government, 308, 309 (graph)

D
Declaration of Independence, 233 (picture)
Delaware Indians, 203–204
Delaware River, 69 (map)
Democracy, 310–311

---

1. In what order are the topics arranged in the index? _____
2. On what pages can you learn about American Indian folklores? _____
3. How many different pages include a graph? _____
4. On what page might you learn how the U.S. President is elected? _____
5. What are the subtopics that fall under the topic *citizens*? _____
6. On which page might you find a picture of an artifact? _____
7. What words are found in parentheses in the index? _____

Name _____   Date _____

Show What You Know

▶ **Directions** Select a nonfiction book with an index. Choose one page of the index to answer each question.

1. What is the subject of the book? _____
2. What is the first and last topic on the page? _____
3. How many subtopics are on the page? _____
4. List one topic and each of its subtopics. _____
   _____
5. What pages can you read to learn about that topic and subtopics? _____

▶ **Directions** Choose four topics or subtopics from the index and look them up in the book. Write a brief summary explaining each topic.

Topic/Subtopic	Summary

Unit 4 Visual Features

Name _____ Date _____

Chart Diagram

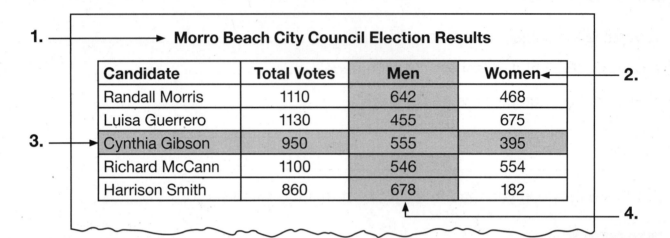

1. → **Morro Beach City Council Election Results**

Candidate	Total Votes	Men	Women
Randall Morris	1110	642	468
Luisa Guerrero	1130	455	675
Cynthia Gibson	950	555	395
Richard McCann	1100	546	554
Harrison Smith	860	678	182

2. ← Women
3. → Cynthia Gibson
4. ← Men column

1. _____
2. _____
3. _____
4. _____

Name _____   Date _____

Understanding a Chart

Charts are a useful way to present information. The **title** is at the top of the chart. It tells the topic of the information given in the chart. The data are arranged by **rows** and **columns**. The rows contain information that goes across. The columns contain information that goes up and down.

In a chart, the **column heading** tells what information is given in that column. See the example on page 50. There are four column headings. They help a reader understand how the information is organized.

▶ **Directions** Use the chart on page 50 to answer each question.

1. How many people total voted in the city council election? _____
2. Which candidate had almost equal numbers of male and female voters? _____
_____
3. Which candidate had the most female voters? _____
4. Which candidate had the most male voters? _____
5. How many females total voted in the city council election? _____
6. Which candidate had the most votes? _____

▶ **Directions** Look at the chart on page 50. Use the words below to label the diagram.

| column | column heading | row | title |

Name _____   Date _____

Using a Chart

Nationwide Calling Direct-Dialed Calls

	Date	Number Called	Where	Time	Rate	Type	Min	Amount
1.	Nov 12	555-555-5332	Bayshore, NY	2:17 P.M.	premium	direct	03	$ .75
2.	Nov 12	555-555-1433	Montauk, NY	3:32 P.M.	premium	direct	10	$ 2.50
3.	Nov 14	555-555-5678	Yonkers, NY	7:28 A.M.	night	direct	42	$ 0.00
4.	Nov 14	555-555-2143	Bayshore, NY	12:42 P.M.	premium	direct	08	$ 2.00
5.	Nov 14	555-555-3200	Bayshore, NY	1:12 P.M.	premium	direct	02	$ .50
6.	Nov 15	555-555-0865	Yonkers, NY	9:32 P.M.	night	direct	33	$ 0.00

▶ **Directions** Use the cell phone bill to answer the questions.

1. What are the column headings on the cell phone bill? _____

2. Which phone call lasted the longest? _____

3. What was the least amount of money spent on a call? _____

4. To where was the shortest call made? _____

5. At what time of day was the 33-minute call placed? _____

6. Based on the bill, which is the least expensive rate for placing calls? Explain your answer.
_____
_____

7. What type of rate was used for the November 15 call? _____

8. What is the phone number of the called placed in Montauk, NY?
_____

9. Based on the bill, what is the premium rate per minute? _____

10. How is the information organized by rows? _____

11. What is the total number of charged minutes (premium) for this bill? _____

12. What is the total amount of this person's bill? _____

Name _____ Date _____

Show What You Know

▶ **Directions** Find a chart in your social studies book. Look at the chart to answer the following questions and to follow the directions.

1. What is the title of the chart? _____

2. What does the chart show? _____

3. How many rows are there? _____

4. How are the rows organized? _____

5. How many columns are there? _____

6. What are the column headings? _____
   _____

7. To whom would this information be useful? _____

8. Write a summary of the information given in the chart. _____
   _____
   _____
   _____
   _____
   _____
   _____
   _____
   _____
   _____

Name _____ Date _____

Map Diagram

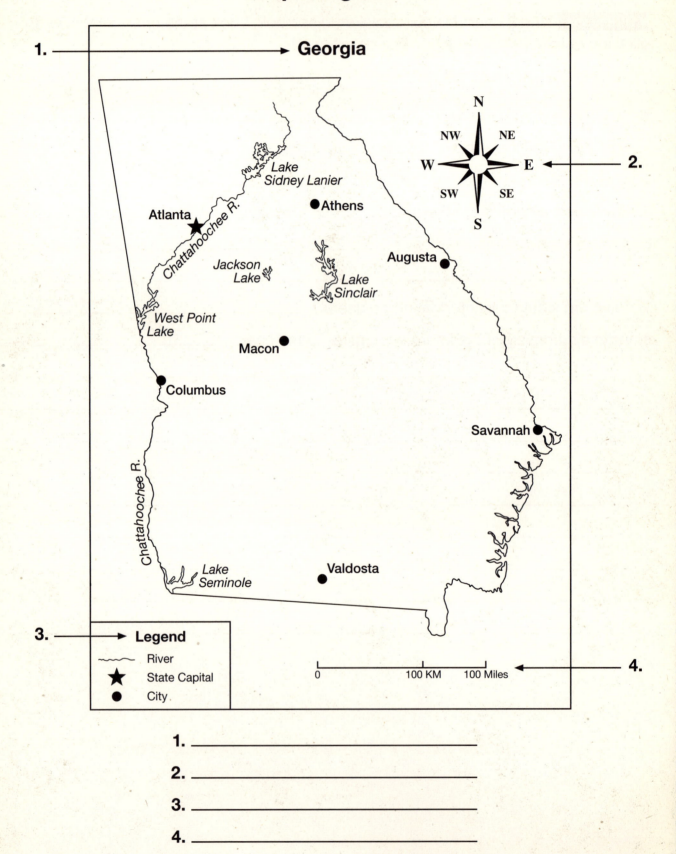

1. _____
2. _____
3. _____
4. _____

Name _____ Date _____

Understanding a Map

A **map** is a drawing of all or part of Earth's surface. The drawing on page 54 is a map of the state of Georgia.

The **title** of the map tells you the place the map shows. A map key, or **legend**, explains what each symbol on a map means. For example, a star on this map stands for the state's capital. The **compass rose** is another special symbol. It shows directions on a map: north **(N)**, south **(S)**, east **(E)**, and west **(W)**. The **distance scale** shows how a particular distance on the map relates to real distance in miles or kilometers.

▶ **Directions** Use the map on page 54 to answer the questions.

1. About how many miles is it from Atlanta to Valdosta? Circle the best answer.

    230   130   400   90

2. Is West Point Lake north, south, east, or west of Lake Seminole?

    _____

    _____

3. What is the state capital of Georgia? _____

4. Which river runs between West Point Lake and Lake Sidney Lanier?

    _____

5. About how many miles is it from Augusta to Savannah? Circle the best answer.

    230   130   400   90

6. Is Savannah to the southeast or the southwest of Atlanta? _____

7. About how many miles is it from Macon to Athens? Circle the best answer.

    230   130   400   90

▶ **Directions** Look at the map diagram on page 54. Use the words below to label the map.

| compass rose | distance scale | legend | title |

Name _____ Date _____

Using a Map

▶ **Directions** Below are five answers. Use the map to write five questions that would give the answer listed.

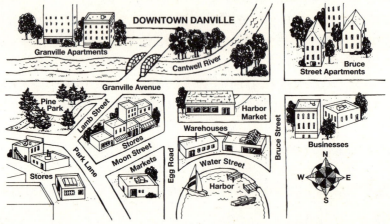

1. _____
   _____ Downtown Danville

2. _____
   _____ Cantwell River

3. _____
   _____ Water Street

4. _____
   _____ east

5. _____
   _____ west

▶ **Directions** Trade your questions with a partner. Create three more questions and answers together.

Question 6: _____

Answer: _____

Question 7: _____

Answer: _____

Question 8: _____

Answer: _____

Name _____ Date _____

Show What You Know

Part 1

▶ **Directions** Use a map of Europe from an encyclopedia or atlas to answer each question.

1. What is the capital of England? _____

2. What is the approximate distance between Madrid and Barcelona? _____

3. What is the relative location of Monaco from Paris? _____

4. In the space to the right, draw the legend that is provided for the map. If the map does not include a legend, create one of your own.

5. Which ocean lies to the west of France? _____

6. In what country is Lisbon located? _____

7. In which direction would you travel if you started in Zurich, Switzerland, and drove to Hamburg, Germany? _____

8. Which three Spanish islands lie in the Mediterranean Sea?
_____

Part 2

▶ **Directions** Assume you are planning a driving tour of Europe. Before you go, you must select seven major cities to visit and use the map's distance scale to determine the approximate distance between each city. Use the chart below to record the cities that you will visit and the approximate distance between them. The city in the *Destination* column of each row will be the same city in the *Starting Point* column in the second row.

Starting Point	Destination	Approximate Distance

Name _____ Date _____

Visual Diagram

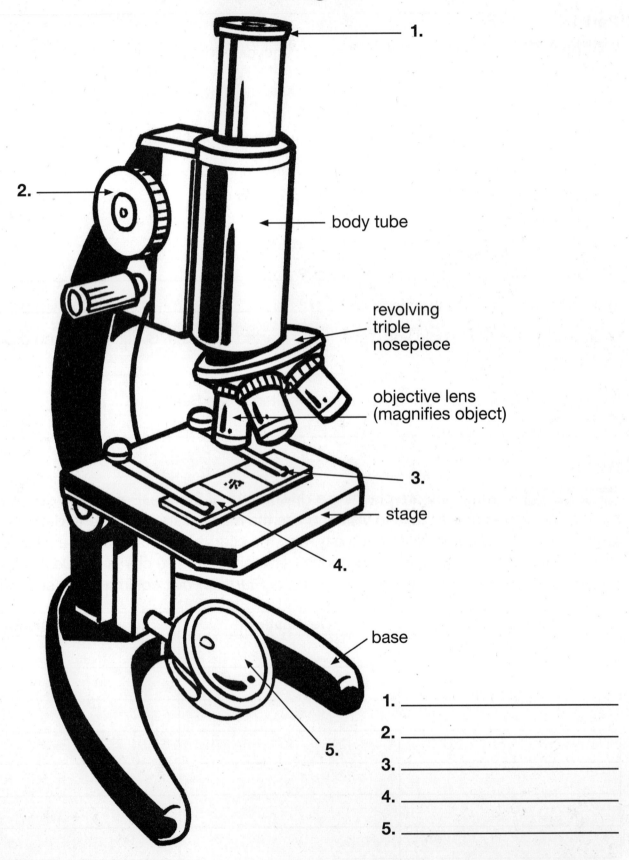

1. _____
2. _____
3. _____
4. _____
5. _____

Name _____ Date _____

Understanding a Visual Diagram

A **visual diagram** is a sketch or drawing that shows the different parts of something. A visual diagram helps a reader better understand how something works or how it is put together. The title tells what is shown in the visual diagram. Labels are used to name the different parts shown in the visual diagram. Lines are used to connect the labels to the parts they name. Read the information below. Then look at the visual diagram on page 58.

Microscopes

A microscope is an instrument with powerful lenses. A microscope magnifies very small things so that they look large enough to be seen and studied. For example, a doctor can study cells in a sample of blood. A drop of blood is placed between two pieces of glass, called a glass slide. The slide is placed on the stage of the microscope and held in place with side clips. The objective lenses magnify the blood sample, which can be viewed from the eyepiece. A mirror below the stage directs light through the sample. A focus knob, on the side of the microscope, adjusts the lenses in the eyepiece to help bring the sample into focus.

The visual diagram shows most of the same information as the paragraph.

▶ **Directions** Look at the visual diagram on page 58. Use the words below to label the diagram.

| eyepiece | focus knob | glass slide | mirror | slide clip |

Name _____ Date _____

Using a Visual Diagram

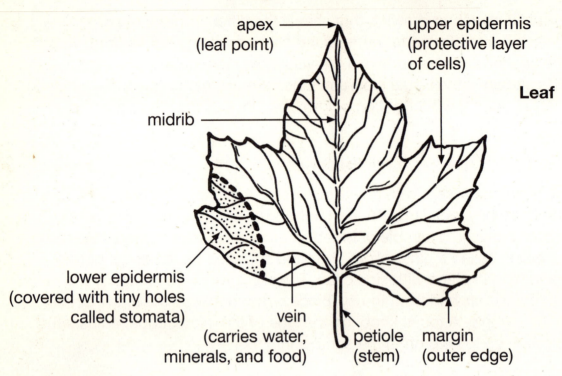

▶ **Directions** Use the visual diagram to answer each question. Write the answer on the line.

1. What is another name for the top point of a leaf? _____

2. What do you call the outer edge of a leaf? _____

3. Which part of the leaf connects to the tree or tree branch? _____

4. What do you call the layer of cells that protects the leaf? _____

5. What carries food and water to the different parts of the leaf? _____

▶ **Directions** Use the visual diagram to write a paragraph about the structure of a leaf.

_____

_____

_____

_____

_____

Name _____ Date _____

Show What You Know

> **Directions** Read the paragraph below. Then draw and label a visual diagram to show the information.

The rain cycle begins with water from Earth's surface, perhaps from a lake or river, rising through the air in the form of water vapor. This process is called evaporation. The water vapor is lighter than the air surrounding it and cannot be seen. The water vapor collects in masses called clouds. Water vapor in the clouds will condense and form drops of rain that are so large and heavy that they fall from the clouds. The rainfall fills the lakes and rivers, completing the rain cycle.

Answer Key

Page 3
1. guide words
2. raised number
3. sample sentence
4. entry word (one syllable)
5. definition
6. entry word (three syllables)
7. pronunciation guide
8. syllable break
9. definition number
10. part of speech

Page 5
1.–20. Answers will vary.
21. state
22. continent
23. day
24. doctor
25. river
26. mountain
27. book or movie
28. planet or god
29. boy or sculpture
30. month

Page 6
1. We
2. He
3. He
4. It
5. they
6. she
7. They
8. it
9. it
10. them
11. them
12. us
13. her
14. us

Page 7
1. be; linking
2. guessed; action
3. is; linking
4. left; action
5. drove; action
6. tasted; linking
7. feels; linking
8. be; linking
9. was; linking
10. sang; action
11. smells; linking
12. worked; action

Page 8
1. more wonderful
2. most beautiful
3. highest
4. deeper
5. biggest
6. largest
7. easiest
8. most unusual
9. stranger
10. most interesting
11. oldest
12. colder

Page 9
Answers will vary. Possible answers are provided.
1. everywhere
2. worriedly
3. Finally, strangely
4. carefully
5. Quickly
6. personally
7. directly
8. there
9. professionally
10. expertly

Page 10
1. it's
2. He'll
3. isn't
4. can't
5. doesn't
6. wasn't
7. aren't
8. They'll
9. doesn't
10. doesn't

Page 11
1. pre
2. non
3. re
4. mis
5. un
6. dis
7. pre
8. non
9. re

Page 12
1. ness
2. able
3. less
4. ish
5. ist
6. less
7. ly
8. er
9. able
10. ish
11. less

Page 13
Sentences will vary.
1. retina
2. optical
3. reflection
4. eyesight
5. pupil
6. organ
7. con-cave
8. con-vex
9. near-sight-ed
10. far-sight-ed
11. cor-ne-a
12. rec-og-nize

Page 14
Sentences and pictures will vary.

Page 15
1. duplicate and Dutch
2. Dutch
3. yes; *during* falls after *duplicate* and before *Dutch*
4. duplicate
5. 3
6. 4
7. made like or exactly corresponding to something else
8. Sentences will vary.

Page 16
1. quaint, quill
2. 10
3. noun
4. 3
5. 2
6. Sentences will vary.
7. quaint
8. No; *quilt* comes after *quill* alphabetically, and *quill* is the last word on this page.
9. quarry
10. quarry
11. Sentences will vary.

Page 17
Definitions will vary.
1. easy to see
2. remarkable or dramatic
3. packed tightly together
4. large and swelling
5. fine particles of mist, steam, or smoke in the air
6. spreads out; gets bigger
7. makes more dense or compact; reduces the volume of
8. tiny drops
9.–10. Answers will vary.

Page 18
1. headline
2. reporter
3. dateline
4. lead paragraph
5. quotation
6. supporting details
7. conclusion

Page 19
Answers may vary. *Sample answers:*
1. A Greenville teacher wins Outstanding Teacher Award.
2. Suzanne Cook, a fifth grade teacher, from James Johnson Elementary School
3. Outstanding Teacher Award
4. last Saturday evening
5. Dr. Marcus Mosby, president of NESTA
6. There were five finalists. Suzanne Cook was presented with $5,000.

7. at the Greenville Manor Hotel
8. She was given the award because she is an outstanding teacher.

Page 20
1. Tigers
2. North Carolina District Nine tournament
3. Monday night
4. Scott Frank
5. Answers will vary and should include one of the following: Peak or Highland Park Elementary Schools or Westlake or Miles Middle Schools
6. Answers will vary. *Sample answer:* "It's great to see the kids so proud of their hard work," said Team Manager Scott Frank of the win.
7. Southwest Little League Advances to Sectionals
8. Answers will vary. *Sample answer:* local news section, sports section
9. Answers will vary. *Sample answer:* Nonfiction; it tells about an event that happened.
10. a staff writer

Page 21
Answers will vary.

Page 22
1. heading
2. graphic
3. name of organization
4. text
5. logo
6. slogan
7. contact information

Page 24
1. www.pineville.gov/recycle
2. cans, bottles and jars; paper; corrugated cardboard
3. Answers will vary. *Sample answer:* metal cans, aerosol cans, plastic bottles with a 1 or 2 on the bottom
4. flatten corrugated boxes and cut them into 2' x 2' bundles
5. Answers will vary. *Sample answer:* newspapers, notebook paper, stationery
6. Answers will vary.
7. Call the phone number and ask, or look on the organization's Web site.
8. You would throw it in the trash.
9. City of Pineville
10. Answers will vary.

Page 25
Brochures will vary but should include a location name, contact information, two graphics, a slogan, two headings, and three bulleted details under each heading.

Page 26
1. topic category
2. topic
3. subtopic
4. page numbers

Page 28
1. Answers will vary. *Sample answers:* states; United States
2. December 29, 1845
3. 23,507,783
4. Bluebonnet
5. Dallas
6. Austin
7. 6
8. 4
9. from a Native American word meaning "friends"

Page 29
1. Answers will vary. *Sample answer:* green on the left half, white on the right half, with a red moon and star in the middle
2. Aphrodite
3. Answers will vary.
4. Answers will vary. *Sample answer:* The richest man in the world for 13 years
5. 1791
6. John Tyler
7. Africa, Antarctica, Asia, Australia, Europe, North America, South America

Page 30
1. headline
2. slogan
3. body
4. illustration
5. persuasive tactic
6. logo

Page 32
1. robot
2. before and after, flattery
3. Answers will vary. *Sample answers:* front page, life section, business section, advertisements
4. Robo Industries
5. Answers will vary. *Sample answer:* that buying the RoboGirl Plus! will make your life better
6. Answers will vary. *Sample answer:* The fine print includes important information that the company doesn't want to point out.
7. Answers will vary.

Page 33
Answers will vary. Ads will vary but should include headline, body, illustration, slogan, logo, and two persuasive techniques.

Page 34
1. tools
2. URL
3. hyperlinks
4. graphic
5. search

Page 35
1. bookstore
2. Store Locator
3. www.booksrus.us
4. Answers will vary. *Sample answers:* to buy a book, to buy a gift card, to find an address of a store
5. free shipping
6. yes

Page 36
1. Answers will vary. *Sample answer:* somebody interested in safety
2. www.besafe.us/bicyclesafety
3. About Us
4. Yes; answers will include 1 of the following: girl on bike, bike hand signals
5. Home
6. Answers will vary.

Page 37
Answers will vary.

Page 38
Answers will vary.

Page 39
1. *An African Adventure*
2. Jack Harrison Smith
3. Sycamore Publishers
4. New York City
5. 1992
6. Yes, the title page shows an illustrator.
7. Jack Harrison Smith (the author)
8. Answers will vary. *Sample answer:* someone who likes adventure books
9. the publisher
10. Answers will vary.

Page 40
Answers will vary.

Page 41
1. a science magazine
2. African Elephants: Looking for a new habitat
3. Coyotes: Moving to a city near you!
4. Monarch Butterflies: Their amazing journey to Mexico
5. 3

Page 42
1. *News Now*
2. Arts in the City: A look at Chicago's growing art scene
3. Letter from the Editor, Top News Stories, A Look at Technology
4. page 34
5. 5–9
6. 2

Page 43
Answers will vary.

Page 44
Answers will vary.

Page 45
1. Answers will vary. *Sample answer:* Police Departments
2. Answers will vary. *Sample answer:* Duties
3. Answers will vary. *Sample answer:* Squad cars help officers cover their territory more quickly.
4. Answers will vary. *Sample answer:* Police History
5. Answers will vary. *Sample answer:* Texas Rangers were organized in 1835.

Page 46
Answers will vary.

Page 47
1. alphabetical
2. 133–134
3. radio, reflection, refraction
4. 4
5. radar
6. 88, 94–95

Page 48
1. alphabetical order
2. 208–211
3. 2
4. Answers may vary. *Possible answers:* 283; 299–301; 308–309; 310–311
5. elections, government, laws, rights of, voting

Page 49
Answers will vary.

Page 50
1. title
2. column heading
3. row
4. column

Page 51
1. 5,150
2. Richard McCann
3. Luisa Guerrero
4. Harrison Smith
5. 2,274
6. Luisa Guerrero

Page 52
1. Date, Number Called, Where, Time, Rate, Type, Min, Amount
2. the third one
3. $0
4. Bayshore, NY
5. 9:32 P.M.
6. night rate; Answers will vary. *Sample response:* The two calls that were made during the night rate had no charge.
7. night
8. 555-555-1433
9. $0.25
10. by date
11. 23 minutes
12. $5.75

Page 53
Answers will vary.

Page 54
1. title
2. compass rose
3. legend
4. distance scale

Page 55
1. 230
2. north
3. Atlanta
4. Chattahoochee River
5. 130
6. southeast
7. 90

6. 206
7. picture, map, graph

Page 56
Answers will vary.

Page 57
1. London
2. 300 miles
3. southeast
4. Answers will vary.
5. Atlantic Ocean
6. Portugal
7. north
8. Mallorca, Menorca, Ibiza

Answers will vary.

Page 58
1. eyepiece
2. focus knob
3. slide clip
4. glass slide
5. mirror

Page 60
1. apex
2. margin
3. petiole or stem
4. upper epidermis
5. vein

Paragraphs will vary.

Page 61
Answers will vary.